BIRDS

ROSE LEWIS

There are many kinds
of birds.
Birds have wings,
feathers, and beaks.

beak

wings

feathers

Some birds can fly.

Some birds cannot fly.

Look at the feathers
on this bird.
Birds are the only animals
that have feathers.
Feathers help birds to fly
and to keep warm.

wing feathers

body feathers

tail feathers

Birds have **beaks.**

Some beaks are round.

Some beaks are sharp.

Some beaks are hooked.

Some beaks are straight.

round

sharp

hooked

straight

Birds like to eat insects, worms, seeds, and fruit. In the winter, it can be hard for birds to find food. Some people like to feed birds in the winter.

Birds lay eggs.
The baby grows
and grows inside the **shell.**
The shell
keeps the baby bird safe.

Birds keep their eggs
warm and safe
by sitting on them.

Some eggs are small.
Some eggs are big.
Some eggs are round.
Some eggs are **pointed**.

pointed

big

round

small

A baby bird
is called a chick.

The chick **hatches**
from the egg.
The chick breaks
the shell with its **egg tooth.**

When the chick hatches
it is all wet!

The chick's feathers dry.
Now the chick is hungry!

beaks

the bill of a bird

egg tooth

a small, sharp tooth used to break out of the egg

hatches

comes out of the egg

pointed

a sharp end

shell

hard outer covering of an egg